Snap books™ Crafts

Fashion Crafts

Create Your Own Style

by Deborah Hufford

Capstone press

Mankato, Minnesota

Snap Books are published by Capstone Press,
151 Good Counsel Drive, P.O. Box 669, Mankato, Minnesota 56002
www.capstonepress.com

Library of Congress Cataloging-in-Publication Data
Hufford, Deborah.
 Fashion crafts: create your own style / by Deborah Hufford.
  p. cm. — (Snap books crafts)
 ISBN 0-7368-4384-1 (hardcover)
 1. Handicraft for girls — Juvenile literature. 2. Dress accessories —
Juvenile literature. 3. Jewelry making — Juvenile literature.
I. Title. II. Series.
 TT171.H75 2006
 646.4'8 — dc22   2005006902

Summary: A do-it-yourself fashion crafts book for children and pre-teens.

Editors: Thea Feldman; Deb Berry/Bill SMITH STUDIO
Illustrators: Lisa Parett; Roxanne Daner, Marina Terletsky and Brock Waldron/Bill SMITH STUDIO
Designers: Roxanne Daner, Marina Terletsky, and Brock Waldron/Bill SMITH STUDIO
Photo Researcher: Iris Wong/Bill SMITH STUDIO

Photo Credits: Cover: Getty Images & Richard Hutchings Photography; 5 Altrendo/Getty Images;
6 (br & tc) PhotoDisc, (bc) Artville, (tr) Ingram Publishing; 7 (c) PhotoDisc; 8 Altrendo/Getty Images;
10 PhotoDisc; (bl) Tim Hicken; 13 Getty Images; 17 PhotoDisc; 23 (l) & 25 PhotoDisc;
28 (bl) Corel, (br) Dover Publications; 29 PhotoDisc; 32 Courtesy Deborah Hufford.
All other photos Richard Hutchings Photography.

Go Metric!

It's easy to change measurements to metric! Just use this chart.

To change	into	multiply by
inches	centimeters	2.54
inches	millimeters	25.4
feet	meters	.305
yards	meters	.914
ounces (liquid)	milliliters	29.57
ounces (liquid)	liters	.029
cups (liquid)	liters	.237
pints	liters	.473
quarts	liters	.946
gallons	liters	3.78
ounces (dry)	grams	28.35
pounds	grams	453.59

Table of Contents

CHAPTER 1

Have a Blast with Fashion Crafts

Get set to become a design queen!

Fashion designers say it's the little touches that make big style statements. Your choice of a belt, a purse, jewelry, or footwear can change your look. This book shows you how to craft special fashion accessories that will make any outfit more exciting.

As you craft, you're sure to come up with creative ideas of your own. Let the designer in you bloom, and soon you'll have dozens of new fashion accessories. Have fun, experiment, and be yourself. That's what fashion crafting is all about.

CHAPTER 2

Play it safe

Safety first, and fun will follow.

You only need a few materials and tools to make the cool crafts in this book. See each project for a list of what you'll need, and always be sure to follow these simple safety rules.

Keep all craft materials and tools away from pets!

* To prevent accidents, keep all craft materials and tools away from pets and young children.

* Always have a grown-up with you when using a hot-glue gun. Make sure the glue gun is not in danger of falling off your work surface. Keep it away from paper, cloth, or anything that could catch fire. Be sure to unplug it when you are finished.

* If you get hot glue on your skin, run cool water over your skin right away.

* Never handle scissors by the blade end. Use them carefully and keep them closed when not in use.

* Always follow directions and work carefully. It's best to take your time and do things safely than to risk having an accident.

REMEMBER!

Safety First
Look for this box throughout this book for safety tips.

CHAPTER 3

Fancy Footwork

You'll flip over these flip-flops.

Design some flowery flip-flops that make a sassy, summer fashion statement. You can do this project using a new pair of flip-flops or a pair you already own. Use your imagination to change plain flip-flops into foot fashion statements.

Here's what you need

* ¼ yard colorful fabric
* scissors
* flip-flops
* 2 silk flowers
* hot-glue gun

Hot Glue Is Way Cool

The best thing about using a glue gun is that the glue cools almost instantly. So while you have to work quickly, you won't have to wait long to wear your new accessories.

Here's what you do

1 Cut fabric into 12 strips that are 1-inch by 6-inches each.

2 Tie three strips to each side of flip-flop straps. Tie each strip once and pull tightly, then tie again for a tight knot.

3 Trim strips to make 1½-inch pieces of fringe.

4 Cut plastic stems off bases of flowers.

5 Put dime-sized amounts of hot glue on center of each toe strap, and attach flower.

Art and Sole

With bright acrylic paints, design stripes, zigzags, dots, or flowers on the edges of your flip-flops.

Goody Two-Shoes

Use beads, charms, ribbons, fancy yarns, buttons, or other goodies to decorate flip-flops.

CHAPTER 4

Hip Fashion

Get hip with these colorful ribbon belts. They're easy to make and oh-so-pretty.

Almost everyone has jeans. But it's how you accessorize them that makes all the difference. Add your own special touch of style with a one-of-a-kind belt you make yourself.

Here's what you need

* jeans
* measuring tape
* 1½ yards ribbon, canvas, or **vinyl** belt material, no wider than 1 inch
* embroidered **decorations**
* scissors
* belt buckle
* hot-glue gun

Design Tip: Your local fabric store should have all kinds of wonderful belt buckles, materials, and decorations for this project.

Here's what you do

1 While wearing your jeans, put measuring tape through belt loops to measure your hips.

2 Add six inches to measurement from Step 1, and cut belt material to this length.

3 Thread two inches of belt material through buckle and form loop, enclosing buckle between two layers of material.

4 Cut a small hole in the middle of the fold of the belt material for the pin of the belt buckle.

5 Hot-glue the layers of material together to secure buckle in place.

6 Cut small belt-buckle holes in the side of the belt that will fit through the buckle.

7 Hot-glue embroidered decorations to belt.

Safety First

To prevent accidents, keep measuring tapes and long pieces of ribbon or other belt materials away from young children and pets.

Happy Endings

Add extra sparkle to your belt by hot-gluing rhinestones on it or writing your name in glitter glue.

CHAPTER 5

Button It Up

Turn an old purse into a terrific tote.

If you're like most girls, you probably have an old purse that you don't use anymore. It might be buried in the back of a closet, or hidden away under your bed. Well, here's a project that will make you want to dig up that forgotten purse or tote bag. By the time you're finished with it, it will look brand new. You'll be glad you didn't throw it away!

Here's what you do

1 Spread buttons on work surface beside purse.

2 Arrange buttons as you like on purse.

3 Using dabs of glue the size of pencil erasers, hot-glue buttons in place.

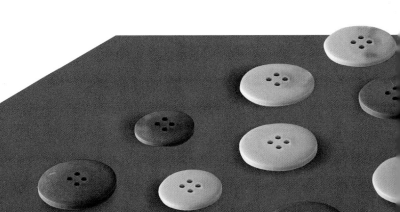

Fashion Grab Bag

Instead of buttons, cover your purse with a variety of charms, pearls, sequins, and even old jewelry.

Design tips If you don't have any old purses, you can buy them at thrift stores or second-hand clothing shops.

CHAPTER 6

Knot to Be Missed

Try knotted bracelets with an exciting new twist.

Yarn isn't just for knitting. You can use it to make beautiful bracelets and a fabulous fashion statement.

Here's what you need

* 1 yard yarn
* scissors
* yarn needle
* beads of your choice

Here's what you do

1 Thread one end of yarn through yarn needle.

2 Double up yarn, and tie a tight knot four inches from the end.

3 One at a time, add beads by threading the needle and yarn through them. Space out beads as you like by tying knots between them. (Be very careful with the yarn needle.)

4 Once you have added all the beads you need for the bracelet length you want, tie a **double knot** after the last bead.

5 Trim strands after last knot to 4 inches.

6 Wrap bracelet around wrist and tie strands in double knot. It should be loose enough that you can slide bracelet off your wrist.

Totally Charmed

Give your bracelet even more dazzle by tying small charms to it.

21

CHAPTER 7

Lend an Ear

These earrings are a snap.

You'll love to show off these fashion statements! From the everyday to the super fancy, you can make fun and flirty earrings as easy as 1, 2, 3.

Here's what you need

* **earring findings**, with **glue pads**
* 2 charms or beads
* hot-glue gun

Here's what you do

1 Dab hot glue on glue pad of one earring finding.

2 Press charm or bead on glue.

3 Repeat for second earring.

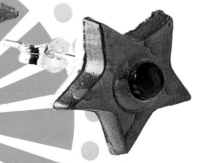

CHAPTER 8

Don't Worry, Bead Happy

Beads are some of the prettiest and most interesting of crafts supplies.

They come in all kinds of different materials like plastic, glass, and metal. You'll find them in all shapes and sizes, and in more colors than you could ever imagine. Pick the beads you really like to make this fun and simple necklace. The beads you choose will say a lot about you and your style.

Here's what you need

* one spool of 18- to 20-**gauge** beading wire
* two dozen large beads, ⅛ to ¼ inches diameter
* four dozen small beads (make sure the holes in the beads are big enough for the wire)
* **hook and eye clasp**
* **needle-nose pliers**
* wire cutters

Here's what you do

1 Decide how long you want your necklace. Have a grown-up use wire cutters to cut a piece of beading wire 6 to 8 inches longer than the size you want.

2 Thread two to three inches of wire through "hook" part of clasp. Knot the wire tightly around it, and use needle-nose pliers to tighten the wire.

3 Cut off excess wire with wire cutters.

4 Start stringing beads onto other end of wire. Create a pattern of large and small beads in the order you like.

5 String the last bead three to four inches from the end of wire.

6 Thread wire through "eye" part of clasp. Knot the wire tightly around the loop of the clasp to secure it.

7 Cut off excess wire with wire cutters.

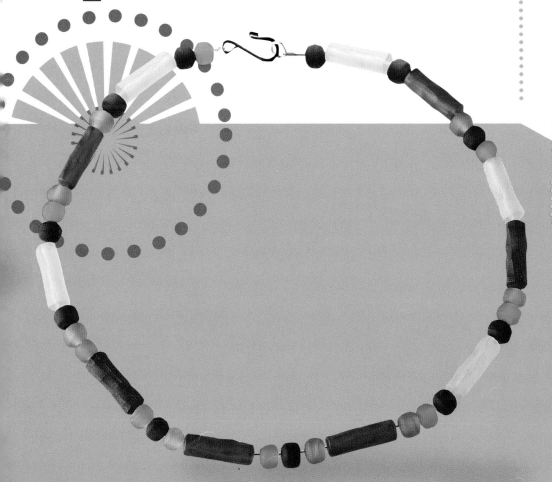

Weave a Colorful Yarn

There are so many wild and wonderful yarns today. Combine yarn with beads for a unique look! Cut a piece of yarn twice as long as your wire. Attach the yarn to the wire, then attach both yarn and wire to clasp. Twist brightly colored yarn around wire. String beads through yarn-covered wire. You'll have a colorful necklace (or bracelet) wrapped in style.

Fast Facts

Fashion Flashbacks

Fashion accessories have been around ever since ancient people hung rocks and shells around their necks. But they weren't common until the 1900s. That's when factories began churning out hats, purses, and jewelry.

"FIT" for Fashion

New York City's Fashion Institute of Technology (called "F-I-T" for short) has one of the world's largest collections of modern fashion accessories. There are over 20,000 items, including jewelry, hats, bags, belts, and shoes.

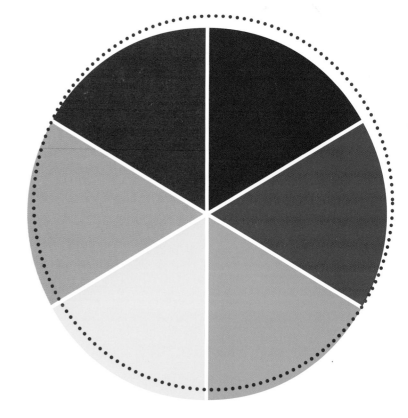

Color Wheel

When making fashion accessories, color is key. This wheel shows how colors work with each other. The colors next to each other work together in harmony. Colors opposite each other have a stronger effect when used together because they have more contrast.

Glossary

accessories (ak-SESS-uh-reez) things that add to an outfit such as jewelry and purses

acrylic paint (uh-KRIL-ik PAYNT) a type of paint used in crafts that dries quickly

decoration (DEK-uh-ray-shuhn) objects that make clothes and accessories prettier and more interesting

double knot (DUH-buhl NOT) a knot that is tied once, then tied again to secure it

earring findings (IHR-ing FIND-ingz) small metal hooks, clamps, or posts used as bases for earrings

gauge (GAYJ) the measurement of wire thickness

glue pads (GLOO PADZ) metal disks on earring findings where jewels or other earring decorations are glued in place

hook and eye clasp (HUK AND EYE KLASP) a type of necklace clasp in which a hook goes through a loop to connect two ends of a necklace or bracelet

needle-nose pliers (NEE-duhl NOHZ PLYE-urz) tool with 2 hinged arms ending in pointed "jaws" that close with hand pressure to grip items

vinyl (VYE-nuhl) a type of very thin plastic that comes in sheets or by the yard

Read More

Bruder, Mikyla. *Bead Girl: 25 Sparkly Beading Projects from Tiaras to Toe Rings.* San Francisco: Chronicle Books, 2001.

The Editors of Klutz. *Simple Sewing: Complete Instructions for 7 Great Projects.* Palo Alto, California: Klutz, 1999.

Maze, Stephanie. *I Want to Be a Fashion Designer.* San Diego: Harcourt, 2000.

Internet Sites

FactHound offers a safe, fun way to find Internet sites related to this book. All of the sites on FactHound have been researched by our staff.

Here's how

1. Visit *www.facthound.com*

2. Type in this special code **0736843841** for age-appropriate sites. Or enter a search word related to this book for a more general search.

3. Click on the **Fetch It** button. FactHound will fetch the best sites for you!

About the Author

Deborah Hufford was a staff writer for *Country Home* and the former editor of *Country Handcrafts* magazine, which included a regular craft column called "Kids' Korner." She was also the crafts editor for *McMagazine,* a magazine created for McDonald's Corporation. Most recently she served as the associate publisher for two of the country's leading craft magazines, *Bead & Button* and *Dollhouse Miniatures*, as well as a book division of crafts titles.

Index